# BANNERS

with Pizazz

written and illustrated by
Diane Guelzow

Resource Publications, Inc.
San Jose, California

Editorial director: Kenneth Guentert
Managing editor: Kathi Drolet
Production editor: Elizabeth J. Asborno
Paste-up artist: Terri Ysseldyke-All
Cover photograph: Perry Chow
Cover production: Huey Lee

Reprint Department
Resource Publications, Inc.
160 E. Virginia Street, #290
San Jose, CA 95112-5848

**Library of Congress Cataloging in Publication Data**

Guelzow, Diane, 1954-
    Banners with pizazz / written and illustrated by Diane Guelzow.
        p.        cm.
    ISBN 0-89390-208-X
    1. Flags.    2. Wall hangings.        I. Title
    TT850.2.G84        1991                                91-40935
    746.3—dc20                                                CIP

5 4 3 2 1 | 95 94 93 92 91

*The verse on page 109 is from "Take My Life," used with permission from Concordia Publishing House, St. Louis.*

# TO THE GLORY OF GOD, THE CREATOR

# Contents

# Illustrations

# Color Plates

# Preface

For as long as I can remember, I have been fascinated with textiles. I enjoyed watching my mother sew for the family. She sewed clothes for us girls; she sewed bedspreads and curtains. Her scraps were never thrown out. Instead they were used for quilts, doll clothes, or just for patches. Her love for textile and her flair for design were an inspiration to me.

My father was a sign painter. Although he did not use fabric in his job, he was gifted in lettering and designing. He was a perfectionist and believed in giving each detail of his work the very best quality.

Surrounded by such artistic abilities and frugality, I absorbed the love for textile and the telling of the message at an early age, and it has been bursting forth ever since.

I wish for you to enjoy this book and to allow it to stir your imagination as you create your messages of life and its joys. Let this book be your tool; use it for inspiration before you begin, for technique as you work, and for praise as you complete your banner! But remember, not even the finest fabric or thread will set your banner apart. You must also know the medium and enjoy the process before it becomes truly worthy of praise.

As a Christian, I see banners as a vital tool in worship. Banners can serve as aids for people who are in need for more aesthetical expressions of faith. If you cannot preach like Paul or sing like angels, perhaps you can create inspiration and joy for others through your banners. It may be your ministry. It will be God's word you are sharing and your talent you are offering! Let your banner do the telling!

# Introduction

Banners are found in many places from car sale lots and open models of new homes to gas stations. We see them fluttering in the sky. They are all eye-catchers. They dazzle in the sunlight and dance in the wind, catching our attention for a moment to convey a quick message. Some of these banners contain certain written messages of sales or grand openings. Other banners contain simple symbols. We are instantly reminded of what the symbols stand for; therefore no written messages are needed.

Banners express a thousand words through a simple symbol or short message. Advertisers know this and use it well to advertise their products. As you drive down a street full of businesses, you can see all the flags, pennants, and streamers. They can literally distract your driving. But they serve their purpose; they get your attention. Therefore, banners and flags are excellent tools for attracting attention.

And why do we want to catch people's attention? There are many reasons, one of which is celebration. Without realizing it, we do want people to notice our celebrations! Some people desire the news to be *big and loud*, while others want to celebrate in a softer, quieter way. Either way of celebrating is appropriate. Here are a few reasons we celebrate.

We celebrate when we want to commemorate an event or occasion. We want to do this in a festive manner! Commemorations include graduations, anniversaries, and birthdays. Personal milestones and accomplishments can be added to the list. Think of some of these kinds of events; the anniversary of the day a person successfully quit smoking might be a perfect reason for celebrating.

Besides personal commemorations, local, state, and national events are worth celebrating. Businesses' anniversaries, Founders Day, State Centennials, and even the Statue of Liberty's birthday are all events worth celebrating. These events of commemoration might be a one-time festival or a week-long jamboree!

Sometimes our celebrations occur when we want to honor someone special: an executive for his many years of dedication to the corporation; a relative or friend who has always stood by you when you were going through some rough times; a grandparent who had guided you through some tough decisions; the retiring teacher who has given years of service to the school district. In honoring someone, we celebrate their courage or strength or friendship or caring. The giver of the celebration decides the reason and sets the stage for the event. Perhaps the giver will want the whole world to know of the occasion or perhaps just a few close friends. Whatever the case, honoring someone indeed calls for celebrating.

Sometimes we celebrate for the sake of tradition. We celebrate St. Patrick's Day whether we are Irish or not. We celebrate President's Day whether we really remember the details of our presidents' lives. Celebrations observed regularly include Ground Hog Day, Valentine's Day, Martin Luther King Jr. Day, Black History Month, and so on. These occasions provide us with awareness and interesting ways of observing some special traditions in our own country and around the world.

Celebrations are found in our homes, schools, and in our places of worship. Some celebrations call for a more reverent festivity, such as baptisms, confirmations, and weddings. Consecration of important vows that are exchanged need the proper setting. However reverent, celebration is taking place.

There are many reasons for celebrating within the church. The Good News is preached and therefore celebration occurs! Not only everyday glory and exaltations are given to God, but higher festivals are celebrated throughout the church year. These call for music, singing, and an array of banners!

Sometimes we want to simply rejoice in life's little happenings. It can include cheering on a winning team, rejoicing in the arrival of spring, or even seeing that your child received an "A" on her report card. The celebrating can contain a hundred people or you alone can be the host and the guest of honor. This kind of rejoicing usually is quickly planned but the event still remains special.

There are other times besides celebrations when we want to catch people's attention. Sometimes we see and hear that people need renewing or refreshing. At times we want others to know how they can be refreshed. That is why so many professionals attend workshops, classes, conventions, and convocations. These places offer ways to refresh people's spirits. People are attracted to organizations that will uplift their tired minds. Just think of all the fanfare at these workshops and conventions. People want to refurbish and restore their confidence. They want to revitalize and rejuvenate their imaginations. They want to strengthen their good skills and motivate their energies! That is why retreats and health clubs do so well today. They offer refreshment from people's hardworking lives.

Sometimes we want to get people's attention to unite them in the same thought or idea. We want people to consolidate their feelings to support the same response. National political conventions serve this idea so well. They serve to unite the party and strengthen their beliefs.

We like to attract attention when we desire commitment. We want promises and support from the people. "Support you local police station" or "Support Amendment 33" are examples of signs you may see around town. We pledge allegiance to our country. We are urged to "Join the Fight Against AIDS." People are encouraged to clean up their streets and to take a stand on gun control. The commitment statements are found all over America, in every media and every sector of life.

There are times when we desire people's attention in a different way. We want to call their attention to things that are more solemn and sacred to us. This might occur at certain solemn times or in special places. A death or a remembrance of an unhappy time in history, such as the Holocaust, calls for a somber moment. It is not the place that is solemn but the occasion. The observance of Passover, Good Friday, and Yom Kippur are other occasions that require solemn attention.

Another time we want to get people's attention is when we desire to inform them. We want to announce, to notify, and to get the message across. This attention getter requires no support or persuasion. It does not try to unite or dissolve. It simply states the facts. An example is an announcement of a school play, choir concert, or an upcoming craft fair.

Whether we need to inform, seek support, or to celebrate, we need to find an appropriate medium to catch people's attention. What are some ways to do this? Smoke riders in planes can announce a message. Pamphlets given out at a store relay a message. Advertisers are everywhere wanting to represent you and your news. That is why there are newspapers, TV and radio commercials, and billboards. That is why there are painters, calligraphers, and layout specialists. Our society drives at getting out the news the fastest, most precise, and up to the minute.

In all these ways and in all these methods, the banner represents the most diversified medium. The banner can be so versatile for so many occasions, for so many places, and for so many age groups. A painted sign is okay, but a banner can dance! A poster in the window is adequate, but a banner can sound with the jingle of bells. A flier announcing a bake sale is sufficient, but a banner can be aromatic with a spray of spices! They can do much more than any other medium.

In summary, banners are catalysts. They cause a reaction. The reaction can be anything from a nod of a head to a complete change of attitude or emotion. Banners can offer your audience much more than any other media by using more body senses than other media. By your selection of the message, the format of your design, and your materials for the banner, you set the stage for your viewers.

Before starting, let's take a quick look at the history of banners.

# The History of Banners

Because banners and flags are such a splendid way of sending a message, and because they can be quickly made, it is no wonder they have been around for over a thousand years!

The Egyptians receive credit for the first flag-like banners. Their banners were simply streamers attached to a staff. The banners were embroidered with emblems of their sacred gods. Feathers were often used on the staffs to represent their pharaohs. Even Egyptian merchants used banners by attaching purple silk flags to their ships.

As years went by, not only did they use fabric, but they engraved ornamental carvings onto their staffs, forming quite elaborate message-makers. The carvings were made out of wood, stone, or metals.

Other nations took up this form of flags and banners. Nations created symbols and embroidered them on all their flags and banners. Ships in the distance, as well as merchants, could quickly recognize ships coming into port from around the world.

Later, about one hundred years before Christ, the Roman military forces used vexillan. Vexilla were square flags that were hung by their upper corners from the crossbars at the top of lances. They were usually red or purple. Eventually, symbols were added to the vexilla.

The first true flags or banners were hung from vertical staffs. One end would fly free while the other end was attached to a bar that kept the flag outstretched. These were used about 700 A.D. These flags would bear the symbols of an empire.

Kingdoms used these banners and flags to serve the same purpose. In travel, the banner announced the approaching king. In war, it marked opposing sides. Even in Disney's renditions of this era, banners are flown in royal pomp and circumstance! Within the walls of kingdoms, banners and flags represented the king, religious beliefs, and royal fanfare. Celebrations and feasts called for their most splendid banners.

The Renaissance Era opened the door for beautiful craftsmanship of the arts. Tapestry and exquisite embroidery were mastered and displayed in the kingdom and throughout the country.

Crusaders and other religious martyrs held their banners high in their Christian warfare. They used their banners to stir emotion and create support for their cause. (See Illustration 1.)

Today, the nations of the world as well as each state proudly fly their flags. Banners and flags have become a perfect catalyst for joining people together for a common cause. This artwork form will stay with us throughout time because it serves its purpose so well.

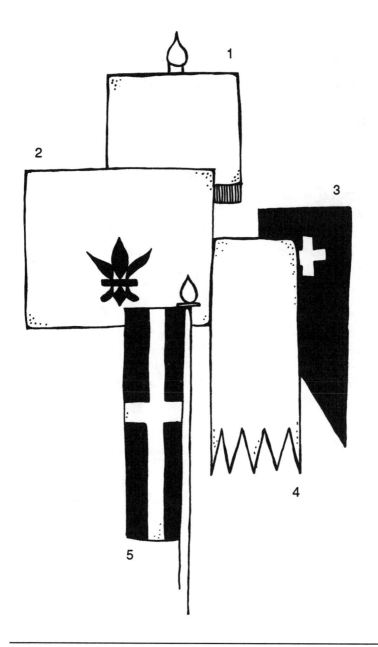

Illustration 1: Flags

1. Roman Vexillum (100 B.C.E.) 2. Charlemagne's Flag (768 C.E.) 3. Crusader's Flag (100 Year War) 4. First Oriflamme (1108 C.E.) 5. Crusader's Flag

# 1.
# THE
# OUTER
# LIMITS
## SIZE
## PROPORTION
## SHAPE

One of the beautiful aspects of banners is the virtually endless possibilities of sizes, proportions, and shapes. These three elements make up the format or background for the message, as does a canvas to a painter. Together they unify and support the message. Although the message itself is the most important element on the banner, it will only be properly transmitted when its size, proportion, and shape are carefully planned. Let us go through each element of these outer limits in order to fully understand the choices available to you.

# Size

Before you begin designing your banner, its size must first be determined. There are basically two sizes of banners: small and large.

Small banners, or personal banners, are usually 2' x 3' and smaller. They are for close viewing by one to four people or even a small gathering. They usually are not processional banners but rather are hung in a permanent position in a room. Occasions for using this type of banner include a small wedding in a chapel or home setting, an anniversary ceremony, reception, baptism, or even a funeral. The small banner can celebrate the moment but can also be kept through the years as a reminder of that special event.

The message or thought on a small banner is personal in nature. I have a small 6" x 6" banner. It was made from a design that my daughter made at a young age. It simply says, "Mom I ♥ U SARA. When I saw her beautiful message, I transformed it into a banner with felt and colorful stitching. It hangs in my office above my worktable. When I'm working late at night or under pressure, that banner relaxes me with family support. It serves its purpose. It's my personal treasure. (See Color Plate 1.)

Recently, I completed a large banner for a convention of five hundred teachers. The banner was 6' x 9'. It was made with felt and adorned with large 1" sequins. My husband suggested that a small-scale banner should be made of the large banner and presented to a retiring executive. So, a small 12" x 18" banner was created, adorned with fancy stitching and ¼" sequins. Thin ribbons and bells were attached to the sides. This banner was presented as a gift, a reminder of a special milestone. It was personalized with much detail (sequins, fancy stitching, ribbons, and tiny bells). Between the two banners, the smaller one definitely allowed for special treatment because it was viewed at a closer range. The details could be seen and appreciated.

On a small banner, colors can be bold and colorful or soft and muted. Pastels work well because they can be seen; their color value is not lost when viewed closely. If pastels are used on a large banner where viewing is distant, both details and soft colors would appear faded and be harder to see. (See Color Plate 2.)

Small banners can be hung in the same way as large banners. Usually they are hung on a wall like a picture. A dowel runs through the top edge to ensure straight hanging. Small banners can also be hung from a banner stand. This is appropriate in the narthex of a church, by a baptismal font, in the corner of a room, or at the entrance of a room. If this free-standing method is used, ribbons and bells can be added to create movement in the draft. Suggested ways of hanging a banner are discussed in chapter six.

Small banners are not recommended for processional movement since the message is more personal and details are kept small. Processing this size of a banner would loose its purpose.

Large banners are for viewing by a large crowd. The size is 2′x 3′ or larger. These banners are for conventions, workshops, congregations, or even parades! Large banners work best in big rooms or outdoors.

In sharing your message with a large assembly, remember that you don't want to start a stampede of people who disagree with your message. The message should create a positive emotion or common goal. It should stir the crowd into support, like a pep rally.

Since these banners are so large, they usually have no place to be hung after the gathering. (Where would you hang a 9' x 12' banner so it does not appear overpowering?) The large 6' x 9' banner I mentioned earlier, which hung in a convention hall, found a permanent home at a church. It hangs on the wall by the choir and organ. Its message, "Make a joyful noise unto the Lord," compliments its location. Determine what will happen to the banner when the occasion is over. Usually large banners are a one-time affair; therefore, you don't want to spend a lot of money on fabrics. Burlap, vinyl, or even paper are more appropriate for the dollar. Because it is viewed in the distance, no one can distinguish the material used.

Likewise, if you are using fabric such as felt or burlap, don't spend needless hours on sewing and placing small details. From the distance your stitching and small details will not be noticed. Instead of sewing on layers of color, try using heat bonding with a fusible fabric. Even a hot glue gun will work faster and save you time. Trying to machine sew on a large banner is difficult with so much fabric. It is better to use a quick running stitch. More about this in chapter four.

A large banner can serve as a background for a convention stage. In this case it is better to hang the banner directly on the wall with tacks or nails. This banner would then be displayed throughout the convention duration.

Large banners can also be processed through a crowd to arouse interest, especially at the beginning of a gathering. It is the movement that stirs excitement. This procession can work well at political or business conventions. Church celebrations, such as Christmas and Easter, are occasions that call for stirring emotions. With the procession of the banner, singing of choirs, and the sounds of instruments, the senses come alive with celebration!

If the banner is processed, a banner rod is needed. A rod is a metal or wooden pole that is attached to the top of the banner, allowing for the banner to be out-stretched. If you are going to use a rod for carrying the banner, extra material needs to be allotted for the top of the banner. (See Illustration 2.)

Therefore, before making your banner, decide how many people will view the banner. Also, decide if your banner is for a one-time occasion. In finding out these answers, you can determine whether your banner's size should be small or large.

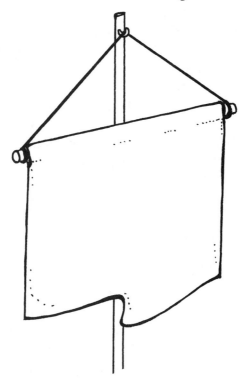

Illustration 2: Banner with rod and cord

# *Proportion*

The proportion of a banner is as valuable as its size and shape. The proportion will incorporate the size you select and guide you in choosing its shape.

The most common proportion of a banner uses a 1:1.5 ratio of the width to the length. This means that the length is 1½ times longer than the width. Take for example a banner that is 24″ wide. The length would be 24″ plus 12″ for a total of 36 inches. This proportion can be hung vertically or horizontally.

Look at the other proportions in Illustration 3. Some proportions are more suitable for certain kinds of messages. These proportions can be reduced or enlarged dramatically. However, it is important to keep the same ratio when increasing or decreasing your size. This requires some calculating before beginning your design. Table 1 lists many proportionate sizes you can use. The figuring has already been done for you.

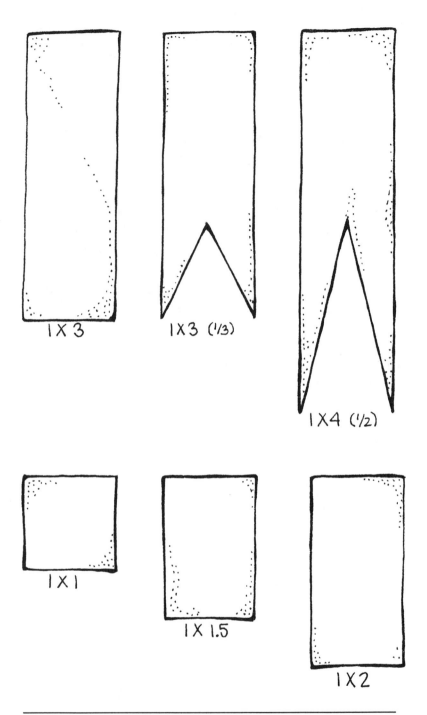

I X 3   I X 3 (¹⁄₃)   I X 4 (¹⁄₂)

I X I   I X 1.5   I X 2

Illustration 3: Banner proportions

## 1 × 1.5 ratio

12" x 18"

18" x 24"
(common size)

24" x 30"
(common size)

2' x 3'

3' x 4½'

6' x 9'

8' x 12'

## 1 × 3 ratio

12" x 36"

18" x 54"

20" x 60"

2' x 6'

3' x 9'

6' x 18'

8' x 24'

## 1 × 2 ratio

12" x 24"

18" x 36"

20" x 40"

2' x 4'

3' x 6'

6' x 12'

8' x 16'

## 1 × 4 ratio

12" x 48"

18" x 72"

20" x 80"

2' x 8'

3' x 12'

6' x 24'

8 x 32'

Table 1: Proportionate sizes

# Shape

As mentioned above, there are two ways a banner can hold a message. Both offer endless possibilities for interesting and powerful backgrounds. A vertical shape is the most common. If a vertical banner is chosen, the words of the message should be small and the message itself should be short or perhaps segmented. The vertical banner often requires the words to be segmented but still remain as a unit. This is challenging, and words often lose their context, making it impossible to read.

With a vertical placement, the viewer's eye will automatically read the message from top to bottom. If words are placed on this kind of banner, the first word or letter should be placed toward the top of the banner, allowing the message to work its way down.

The other common shape for a banner is horizontal. This is a great shape if the message is long or consists of one long word. Using small letters, it is possible to sew an entire sentence across the width of the banner. In this way the viewer will read the message from left to right. The placement of the message should follow the same guidelines as in the vertical position. (See Illustration 4.)

The shape of the banner is the last element to consider before beginning the layout of your design. It is just as important as the other two elements and will play a valuable role in forming the background for the banner. There are too many dull-shaped banners that repeat the vertical rectangular look. Artists can make an exciting statement by developing new shapes. The possibilities are only limited by your imagination! (See Color Plate 3.)

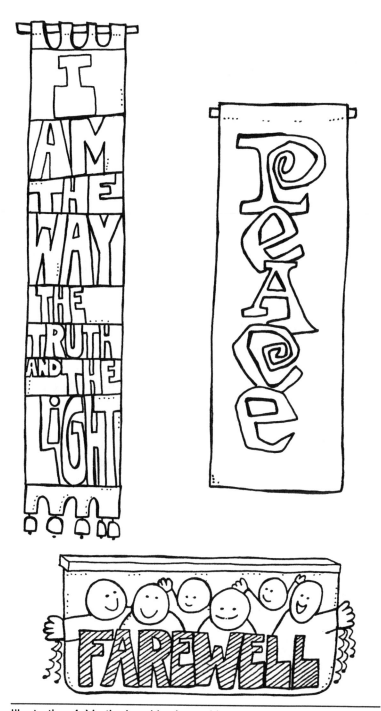

Illustration 4: Vertical and horizontal banners

With all banner shapes, the most important consideration is allowing enough room for the message. So the size, proportion, and shape have to work together before any cutting of fabric takes place. When the size of the message works together with the proportion you have in mind, the remaining empty space can present many interesting possibilities!

Let's start with the most common rectangular shape. Take your message (and symbol if you have one) and place it within the rectangular shape. The message can be placed horizontally, vertically, diagonally, or even in a broken pattern. The first step in finding a new and interesting shape is to consider cutting into the top and/or the bottom of the original rectangle. (See Illustration 5.)

Keep in mind that a dowel will run through the top of your banner. You can slip it through some or all of the fabric, but only a minimal amount of extra fabric is needed. Therefore, some creative cutting can be done in this location. Most banners are made out of felt, a perfect fabric for cutting because it will not unravel. Cuts can be rectangular, V-shaped, or semi-circular in shape. These can be one big cut or smaller repeated patterns.

If the tops of banners are created with these interesting cuts, it is visually pleasing to repeat the top design along the lower edge. Look at the illustrations again. Even without the message, the banner silhouette is aesthetically balanced. It is as though you have cut out a design from the top of the banner and placed it along the bottom edge. As you begin with a rectangular sketch, simply cut out a top border and trace the cut-out portion on the bottom edge. You'll be off to a good start!

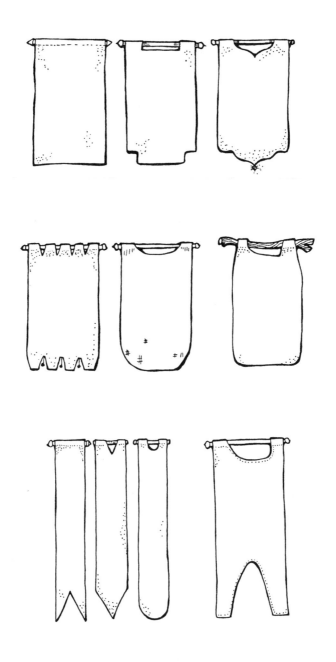

Illustration 5: Banner shapes

21

Now consider another possibility. Any extra space along the bottom edge can be cut into, forming ribbon-like dangles. These dangles are not added on to the main piece but are cut out of the main piece. These shapes work well for processional banners because they dance their message to spectators. (See Illustration 6 and Color Plate 4.)

One more possibility is to cut out the fabric, creating a window effect. This can be done on letters that are closed in (o, e, b, d, p, q, g, a). Once again, felt works ideally since it will not unravel. You may also cut out shapes that add to the mood of the message, such as hearts, moons, suns, or crosses. (See Illustration 7.) Take, for example, a banner dealing with the message of love. You could cut out hearts along the sides and lower edge. Within the windows you could

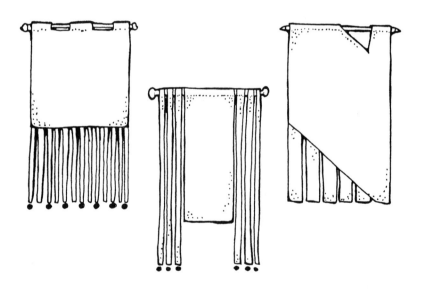

Illustration 6: Dangles

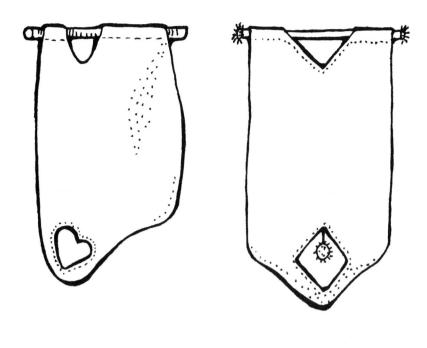

Illustration 7: Banner cutouts

hang some bells. If the banner is processed through a congregation, you might place photos of its members in the openings.

Illustration 8 shows another idea along that line. Make two layers of felt, each the same shape. In the first layer, cut out appropriate shapes. Place that layer on top of the background layer, creating a see-through effect that reveals a bright color behind the cutouts.

The possibilities are indeed limitless. Before we end on this topic, two contemporary ideas must be shared.

Most banners are two-dimensional. Why not create a three-dimensional banner? They are just as easy to make and a lot more dynamic! They are more appropriate for joyous occasions because they can dangle, spin, and twirl! Viewers can read them easier because you can repeat the message on more sides. Thoughts

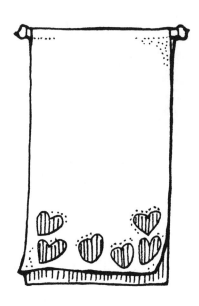

Illustration 8: Overlapping cutout

that cannot be broken down to one word are better expressed on a multi-sided banner. Consider a banner celebrating the Trinity. One side can be for the Creator, another side for the Redeemer, and a third side for the Holy Spirit.

A circular banner twirls around as it is processed down an aisle. Circular banners turned into vibrant rainbows generate a feeling of hope and God's love. The story of Pentecost with the wind and fire can be depicted with red, yellow, and orange streamers. The wind effect is created by the movement of the air as the banner is processed. Windsocks are also delightful dancing banners that work well indoors as well as outdoors. Three-dimensional banners are definitely processional banners. (See Illustration 9.)

Finally, another contemporary banner style leaves quite an impression on its audience. A three-dimen-

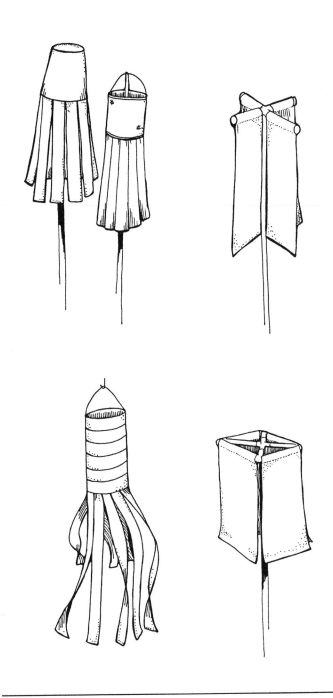

Illustration 9: Three-dimensional banners

sional banner can take a shape beyond rectangles and circles. An excellent shape would be that of a doll. Doll shapes are great for the classroom, the church, or even as a gift for a friend who needs to remember something important. This doll shape can be ten inches tall or lifesize. I once had a group of teenagers create several thirty-inch dolls. They sewed the dolls and decorated them in contemporary clothing. We then attached them to a cross made out of wood. On the cross was the statement, "Hang on to the Word of God." (See Color Plate 5.)

Other doll shapes could be lifesize dolls that are large enough for a child to cuddle with. A message of "I'll listen to you" creates a special corner in a bedroom or classroom. As long as there is a message being communicated, it's a banner.

That rectangular banner shape now seems a little overused, doesn't it? The sky is the limit. The only one holding you back from creating the very best is yourself, and we haven't even gotten to the message part of the banner yet!

2.
THE
INNER
LIMITS
ELEMENTS OF
DESIGN
SYMBOLS
LETTERING

Now let's explore what you can do with the inner dimensions of the banner. Basically the interior message contains one or two features, a message, and/or a symbol. We will, therefore, take a look at some beginning steps of creating a quality design.

One of the first steps in design is to have some working knowledge of the elements of design. The elements of design consist of the five foundations of quality art: line, shape, value, texture, and color. When these elements work together, the artwork appears complete.

In considering the message, symbol, and general layout of your banner, it is important to give each of these elements of design some attention. They can appear balanced (no element dominates another element), or one element can be stressed to create a unique effect. Let's explore each element and discover its contribution to the total design.

# Line

A dot or a dash can be the simplest example of line. Lines can be short, fat, or straight. They can be broken or jagged, bent or twisted. They can intersect or run parallel. Lines can divide, merge, or weave together. They can ascend or descend. They can express emotion with a single curve upward or downward.

Lines are everywhere in nature. You see bare tree branches waving in the air. Curling lines of a grapevine wrap around woven lines of fencing. Jagged lines of the ocean tide are sketched in the sand with each movement of the surf. The zebra displays her lines majestically, while the cat shyly hides her curling tail.

Once you witness the lines around you, you can see that lines are suggestive. A curved-up line suggests happiness, while a line turned downward represents sadness. A divided line suggests decisions. Woven lines represent harmony or unity. Each time you begin a design for your banner, keep in mind some of these representational associations with lines.

In art, lines are found in letters and symbols. As you create these lines with your lettering and symbols, you can emphasize them with yarn, ribbons, machine stitching, and so on. Tassels and streamers can be made to emphasize lines. Loosely woven fabrics, such as burlap, can have some of its threads pulled out to create open lines in the banner. Those new spaces can be rewoven with ribbons or yarn.

In Illustration 10, the stems are emphasized because they cover the largest area on the banner and then are lengthened into streamers for the banner. The other elements of design are present, but the element of line is dominant.

# Form or Shape

When a line touches itself, it creates a form, also called a shape. There are many common shapes that we learned in school, such as circles, triangles, squares, rectangles, diamonds, and polygons. If you recall geometry, you may know of more complicated shapes.

Think for a moment of how society uses these shapes as symbols. A stop sign takes the shape of an octagon. A yield sign takes the form of a triangle. A heart shape represents love.

Such forms are used in art. The background shape of your banner should be an interesting eye catcher. In the previous chapter, you decided which background shape to use. Now you can consider some shapes for

Illustration 10: Line

the inside of the banner. Consider which shapes leave a message all by themselves (heart, arrow, circle). These shapes can be glued on, sewn down, stuffed, and even painted on. They can be flat or three-dimensional. They can be made of fabric, plastic, or wood. When you think of shapes on your banner, consider how you can make your shapes communicate a message.

The banner in Illustration 11 emphasizes shape with the use of stars. Some are cut out of the fabric, while others are added on to the banner. Sequins emphasize their presence even more. These shapes are the dominating element of this banner.

Illustration 11: Shape

# Value

Value can be explained in terms of light, dark, bright, or dull. In other words, how does light affect the art form? This is an important element of design.

Everyday you see and experience the importance of value. In our environment we see bright clouds against a darkened sky, dark seeds in a brilliant watermelon, and shadowy shapes on the sidewalk. Creation shows us beautiful combinations of light and dark and everything in between. Even as you dress and decorate your house, you use light value. You wear white pearls against a black dress. You brighten your wardrobe with bright accents such as scarves and belts. In your house you display accent colors that draw attention to a lovely couch or an interesting window design. Each room contains accent areas of brightness, softness, or dullness.

As you think about your world and your designs for your banners, imagine them as a black and white picture. In this way, it becomes easier for your eyes to see light and dark and the contrast of the two. A good piece of artwork has a balance of light and dark. When you plan your banner design, ask yourself which areas of your banner will be highlighted and which areas will be more subdued. Your banner can consist of a dark background with lighter colors for the lettering and symbol. Or it could be the reverse, where the background is light and the lettering and symbol are darker. You can also add values of colors between light and dark. This will keep your design well-balanced visually and aesthetically. (See Illustration 12.) More about shades and tints in the section about color.

# *Texture*

Texture is the surface feeling of an object. Everything in this world has some sort of texture. The surface of an object can be rough, smooth, scratchy, prickly, bumpy, soft, hard, silky, sandy, slippery, or gooey, to name a few.

In the manufacturing world, spinoffs from nature's textures are created. The clothing industry creates wardrobes of textured articles from alligator shoes to feathered hats, from glassy purses to bumpy furs. Leather jackets go well with silky scarves, and camelhair coats complement shiny jewels. Even in our homes, we find an array of textures from wood paneling to wool blankets, satiny bedsheets to fuzzy

Illustration 12: Value

bathtowels. Textures create interesting shadows, giving depth and value to the things around us. Textures appear differently depending on the lighting.

Too often, texture is overlooked in the creation of a banner, and the artist will make her banner completely out of the same fabric. When you plan your banner, think about its surface area. Will you make your banner completely out of the same fabric, or will you use a variety of fabrics?

In either case, you can make your banner stand out with a few added touches that offer more textures. If your banner is made completely out of the same fabric (felt, for example), consider some ways of adding to the focal point (the message or symbol) of the banner. At this location you may wish to add some sequins, ribbons, beads, or embroidery stitches. You may even build up your focal point by putting a little stuffing underneath the lettering or symbol. This raised look, with the proper lighting, will create some depth. Squeeze-bottle paint can be added on to the banner around the focal point. This paint can be purchased in a fabric store in a large variety of colors and thickness, and even with glitter mixed in with the colors. Further, sequins and beads can be pressed into this paint.

Textures can be found in a number of fabrics. The two most common for banners are felt and burlap. Each of these offers its own kind of texture. Use them separately or together. Silk and muslin are other good textures that can play together in creating your banner. Even with a combination of fabric, you can still add depth to your banner with the addition of pom pons, tassels, ribbons, and so forth. More about this later.

Textures add life and interest to the banner by giving it depth. In Illustration 13, you can see the burlap background, satiny ribbons, feathers, and shiny bells. Together, they create a balanced message.

Illustration 13: Texture

# Color

Color is the finale of design. It is as emotional and personal as an individual. Color can communicate any emotion from anger to peacefulness, from sadness to jubilation. In nature color communicates emotion through the seasons. Each season displays its beauty through the colors of flowers, grass fields, sky, trees, and leaves.

In creating your banner, this element will be your strongest tool for the feelings you wish to translate to your audience. You must use it with caution, for your choice in color can contradict the message or create an altogether different feeling toward your message.

It is important, therefore, to know color and the color wheel. You will refer to it often as you choose colors for your banner. A color wheel is a diagram that displays primary and secondary colors and how they are related and formed from one another. Some color wheels even display all colors that are created from one another. These are complicated but most helpful. You can purchase one from any art supply store.

A color wheel begins with three main colors, known as the primary colors. They are red, blue, and yellow. From these three, all other colors are formed. If you take two primary colors and blend them together, you will create a new color. For example, red and yellow create orange; red and blue create violet (purple); and yellow and blue create green. Green, violet, and orange are known as secondary colors, having been formed from the primary colors.

The color wheel becomes more interesting when primary colors are blended with secondary colors. Look carefully at the color wheel (Color Plate 7) and study the newly formed colors. Yellow (P) and green (S) form yellow-green; yellow (P) and orange (S) create yellow-orange. Red (P) and orange (S) form red-orange; red (P) and violet (S) create red-violet. You can see a pattern developing around the color wheel. Colors continue to develop by mixing the colors around the wheel. (See Color Plate 6.)

In creating a banner, the use of color is an important concern. It is the first distinction a viewer will notice, and it will leave the first impression.

With a better understanding of color, you will discover that some colors don't get along visually, while others together work in perfect harmony. Some people are aware of this factor instinctively; others have trained themselves to observe this important detail. The following section will be a helpful tool. Learn the terms and how they can assist you.

For a banner with a strong, enthusiastic message, use colors that are opposite on the color wheel. Another term for "opposite" in reference to the color wheel is "complementary." One set of often-used complementary colors is red/green. These two colors are strong and vibrant. Other complementary sets include orange/blue and yellow/violet. Many schools choose these colors because they are bold and enthusiastic. They are great on banners where the necessary impact is power and boldness.

To support a softer message that remains colorful but not as powerful as complementary colors, use analogous colors. Analogous colors are colors that appear side by side on the color wheel. Examples of analogous colors are yellow, yellow-orange, orange, and red-orange. Green, green blue, blue, and blue violet are also analogous. Three, four, or even five side-by-side colors can be chosen. These colors work together as a team, supporting a message well and creating a harmonious appearance. (See Color Plate 7.)

Another arrangement of working colors is known as a split complementary. This arrangement uses three colors. One of the colors is at the extreme end of the color wheel and the split refers to the colors on both sides of its complementary color. Take for example orange. Its complement would be blue, but in forming its split complementary, you would use the colors on each side of the blue: blue-green and blue-violet. So your colors form a split: orange, blue-green, and blue-violet. These colors create a powerful message and can be used well for a message that needs color support.

Sometimes a softer color support is needed. In that case, you might want to consider tints and shades of colors. Tinting is adding white to a color on the wheel. Red turns into pink, blue into light blue, and so on. Tints are usually used for lighter messages.

Adding black to a color is called shading. A shade is a darker form of a color. Red turns into maroon, blue turns into navy or dark blue. You can create a color arrangement of the shades and tints of one color (white, pink, mauve, red, deep red, maroon, and black). This works well for a message that has a softer tone. Likewise, you could use the tint and shade of two colors and create many new colors. (See Color Plate 8.)

These possibilities offer the artist a precise tool to make her decisions easier. But for the adventurous artist, there is another facet to consider when working with color.

Colors have many symbolic connotations throughout the world. Colors are emotional, and certain emotions have been attached to each color imaginable. If you wish to attract your audience through emotion, you may consider using certain colors that traditionally have certain connotations about them.

Yellow — a warm color suggesting happiness and cheerfulness. It is a color of intelligence and purity.

Orange — a blend of red and yellow, creating mixed feelings. It is a warm but fiery color, full of energy and life. It is a color of success and pride.

Red — a powerful color that demands attention. It is a fighting color as well as a passionate color. Red can suggest anger and rage. Red stands for blood and danger.

Purple — a cool color. It always has been a color of royalty and power, of dignity and strength. Purple is a color of wealth and passion.

Blue — a color of quiet strength. It is a calm color like the sky or a flowing stream. It is a relaxing color that reflects truth and a right spirit. It can be sad and weary, sometimes depressing.

Green — symbolizes growth and a spirit of hope. It is an inspirational color as well as a refreshing color. Green is a color of renewal or rebirth of energy.

White — the presence of all colors. It has always symbolized purity and innocence. It suggests peace and pardon. It offers surrender.

Gray — halfway between white and black. Symbolically, it is caught in the middle, a color that cannot be trusted. Gray is a doubting color, a neutral color. It does not belong to any other color and therefore doesn't take sides. It suggests humility and offers no resistance.

Black — the absence of color. It suggests impurity and sinfulness. It suggests guilt, death, and sadness. Black represents depression and utter despair. However, when black is used as a background for bright colors it displays a powerful strength!

Brown — a neutral color. It does not commit one way or the other. It is neither a strong color nor a weak color. It is a color of soil and therefore can suggest support.

Gold — a color for wealth. It suggests extreme gladness. It sparkles in the sun and radiates in all directions. It is a warm and metallic color. It is a valuable and treasured substance.

Silver — not as precious as gold, but still a valuable symbolic color. It, too, sparkles, but to a quieter color scheme. Think of silver sparkling stars against a black background. It is a delicate color as well as a color of strength, like that of armor and a sword.

These color associations are listed in Color Plate 9 for quick reference.

Note that colors can be warm or cold. For example, yellow, orange, and red are warm while blue, green, and purple are cold. When setting a mood for your audience, consider this option.

You are now acquainted with the elements of design. When you plan your banner, be sure to address each of these elements. Remember, you can use them in complete balance or make one element more dominant than another. As you continue to create banners, you will work through these elements of design more quickly. For now, carefully plan out how each element will work together to create the most uniform message.

Color Plate 1

A personal message

Color Plate 2

Top: Pastels work best for close viewing.
Bottom: Bold colors for distand viewing.

Color Plate 3

Vertical and horizontal banners

Color Plate 4

Above: Dangles
Opposite: Cutout bottoms

Color Plate 5

Three-dimensional doll banner

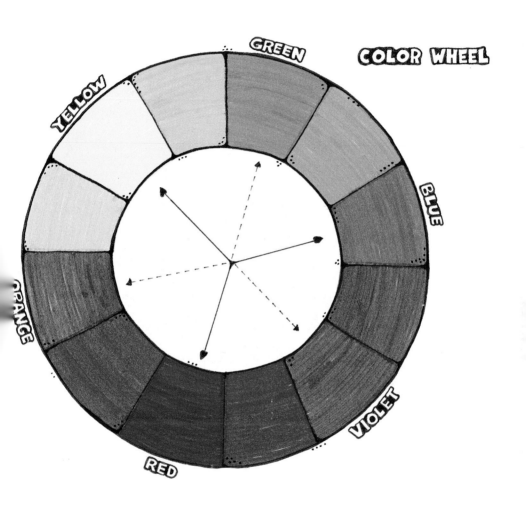

Color Plate 6

Color Plate 7

Top: Complementary
Bottom: Analogous

Color Plate 8

Top: Split complementary
Bottom: Shades and tints

# COLOR ASSOCIATION

 Yellow — a warm color suggesting happiness and cheerfulness. It is a color of intelligence and purity.

 Orange — a blend of red and yellow, creating mixed feelings. It is a warm but fiery color, full of energy and life. It is a color of success and pride.

 Red — a powerful color that demands attention. It is a fighting color as well as a passionate color. Red can suggest anger and rage. Red stands for blood and danger.

 Purple — a cool color. It always has been a color of royalty and power, of dignity and strength. Purple is a color of wealth and passion.

 Blue — a color of quiet strength. It is a calm color like the sky or a flowing stream. It is a relaxing color that reflects truth and a right spirit. It can be sad and weary, sometimes depressing.

 Green — symbolizes growth and a spirit of hope. It is an inspirational color as well as a refreshing color. Green is a color of renewal or rebirth of energy.

Color Plate 9

White — the presence of all colors. It has always symbolized purity and innocence. It suggests peace and pardon. It offers surrendering.

 Gray — halfway between white and black. Symbolically, it is caught in the middle, a color that cannot be trusted. Gray is a doubting color, a neutral color. It does not belong to any other color and therefore doesn't take sides. It suggests humility and offers no resistance.

 Black — the absence of color. It suggests impurity and sinfulness. It suggests guilt, death, and sadness. Black represents depression and utter despair. However, when black is used as a background for bright colors it displays a powerful strength!

 Brown — a neutral color. It does not commit one way or the other. It is neither a strong color nor a weak color. It is a color of soil and therefore can suggest support.

 Gold — a color for wealth. It suggests extreme gladness. It sparkles in the sun and radiates in all directions. It is a warm and metallic color. It is a valuable and treasured substance.

 Silver — not as precious as gold, but still a valuable symbolic color. It, too, sparkles, but to a quieter color scheme. Think of silver sparkling stars against a black background. It is a delicate color as well as a color of strength, like that of armor and a sword.

Color Plate 10

Banner idea from clip art

# Symbols

## Realistic Symbols

Visual expression is one of the earliest forms of communication, existing before written language. Early Egyptians drew symbols to record their life story. Before them, cave dwellers recorded their hunts with inscriptions on cave walls. Visual expression is a representational form of communication. It has been and will remain an indispensable tool for telling. Visual expression reaches more people quicker than written language. Some symbols surpass cultural and language barriers. (See Illustration 14.)

Symbols are the soul of communication in art. They offer rest from the written form, and they allow us to aesthetically read a message. Banners can team up with this style of communicating and offer its audience a new and exciting way to receive a message. Long messages may be expressed with a symbol, eliminating words but still communicating.

Symbols can be copied from our environment: a sun symbolizes hope and light; a rainbow, promise; a star, pride and guidance; an apple, knowledge; a tear, sadness; a heart, love and passion. You can find many books on symbols for the church, nature, society, etc. Many businesses select a symbol (logo) based on their product and service.

Symbols express a deeper meaning that others can identify with. For example, a cross is a universal symbol. It consists of a vertical line and an intersecting horizontal line. The cross used in the crucifixion manifested the reality of God's love; therefore, the cross is the most endearing symbol to Christians.

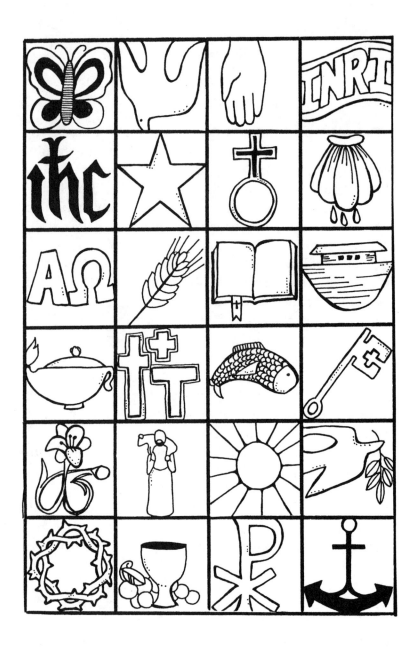

Illustration 14: Symbols

You may wish to use a realistic picture on your banner. You can draw this by hand and reconstruct it with fabric. Sometimes you might be given a picture to put on the banner. In these cases you are trying to achieve exact reproductions on your banner. In chapter four we will discuss how to enlarge a design or a given picture.

## Abstract Symbols

You may desire an abstract symbol on your banner—something that will require your audience to look at it for a while in order to fully understand the message. Many artists prefer this method of abstracting the realistic in order to arouse the audience's attention.

New symbols can be created by simplifying a realistic picture. Picture in your mind an apple as realistically as you can. Now begin to simplify it by finding its closest geometric shape, a circle. Simplify the stem and leaf by adding a thick line and an oval. Now you have an abstraction from a realistic form. Many other new symbols can be created in this same fashion. (See Illustration 15.)

You will find this method quite easy to do, especially if you cannot draw realistically. When you look for the proper symbol for your message, think beyond an object. Think of its symbolic meaning (for example, a dove stands for peace and hope; a sword for anger or vengeance). You'll be surprised how many appropriate symbols you will come up with.

If you have been approached to make a banner, inquire if there is a particular symbol, design, or logo that should be used. This will save you time in creating one of your own. Sometimes organizations want

43

their logo to be used, while others might want a theme of the gathering to be symbolized.

## Other Symbol Ideas

Greeting cards offer many idea starters for use in banners. It is a good idea to start a file of greeting cards with interesting designs that could be used later in a banner. I spend more money on cards to keep than on cards to send! A card may be selected because its color combination is interesting to you, or perhaps the design caught your attention. Wedding cards, children's cards, baptism cards, and Jewish holiday cards are appealing for banner possibilities. Use the parts of the card that are the most helpful for you. Change or add to the parts to create a banner design that serves your objective. The symbol design found in Color Plate 10 evolved out of a greeting card. It started as a simple picture but was transformed into a beautiful felt banner for a classroom. Both parents and

Illustration 15: Abstraction

children enjoyed seeing this symbol of a caring class-room.

If creating your own design is a difficult chore, here is another possibility. School and church offices often have catalogs of symbols, logos, and activity designs that they print onto their newsletters and bulletins. These designs offer beautiful messages with both lettering and symbols. Illustration 16 shows two banners designed from clip art. You may change or add to the design to fit your idea of shape, size, and coloring of the banner.

Now you probably have many ideas for your banner design. Investigate your resources through books at the school or church office. The public library offers books on symbolism from all faiths. Embroidery books, church history books, history books, and other banner-making books will assist your planning. It is important to keep a collection of your own ideas as well as copies of designs you've seen. This will give you a first-step reference to look at when you are ready to create a new banner.

Illustration 16: Ideas from clip art

# Lettering

In the beginning of this chapter, I shared with you the basic information on the elements of design. This background knowledge enables you to work within the inner limits of the banner, using both letters and symbols with quality craftsmanship. As your idea develops from collected information (what your banner is to say, how many people will be seeing it, colors that are to be used, etc.), you can begin to sketch some ideas down on paper. I always work with a tablet of graph paper. In this manner, I can quickly draw outside shapes, lettering, and symbols. The size might develop as I draw all the inside information, or I might start off with a required size. Dimensions can be scribbled in at a scale that is comfortable to work with. Once you begin to determine measurements and the banner shape that will carry the message comfortably, you can begin to position your lettering and symbol. (See Illustration 17.)

In considering how and where you will position the message and symbols, you must first determine which of the two will be the focal point of the banner. Of all the things we have discussed so far, it is the message and the symbol that are the most important parts of the banner. All the other items support the message. It is with these two areas that new decisions have to be made. The lettering and the symbol need to work together as a team.

## Dominant Lettering

Dominant lettering occurs when you make the lettering the prominent (larger) part of the total layout, keeping the symbol quieter (smaller). When the ban-

47

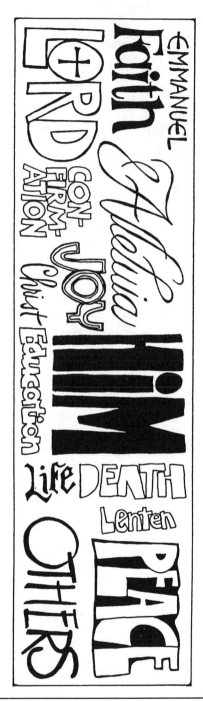

Illustration 17: Lettering

ner is viewed, the audience will first see the written message and then notice the symbol. The words "Christ is Risen" is a message you would want to make larger since it is such a dramatic and important statement. A symbol of a rolled-away stone or Easter lilies may accompany the words but on a smaller scale. Illustration 18 shows the words, "You are special," which is indeed an important message; therefore, the letters are larger than the symbol of the children. Together, the lettering and the symbol work together to create a balanced message.

## Equally Balanced Lettering

Another method of using lettering and symbol is to make both the same size, rendering them equal in importance. Neither overpowers the other. Illustration 19 depicts a banner designed for a community to vote on building a public pool. The written message says "Vote yes," and the other half of the banner shows refreshing water. The "yes" message or the refreshing

Illustration 18: Dominant lettering

colors of the water may cause someone to vote for building the pool. Together, the equal size supported the total feeling of the message.

## Submissive Lettering

If the written message can be understood better through a symbol, then the symbol should be larger than the lettering. For example, a beautiful rainbow in bright colors and multi-colored sequins is a dominant symbol over smaller lettering stating, "God's promises are forever." Here the rainbow directly symbolizes God's covenant and promise. By seeing the symbol first, the message is understood. The lettering just enhances it. Illustration 20 displays the beautiful architecture of St. Louis. The symbols identify the city and its landmarks; the written message defines it.

These three layout patterns will work well for many kinds of banners. Remember, with each of these patterns you can still emphasize your focal point with the use of colors. For less dominant areas, use neutral col-

Illustration 19: Equally balanced lettering

Illustration 20: Submissive lettering

ors that blend into the background color. This will quiet down that area. In contrast, the dominant area should have colors that stand out or are brighter.

## Letter Types

When considering lettering for your banner, you will discover thousands of typefaces along with varieties of letter sizes. Illustration 21 shows four types of lettering. Let's consider one method at a time.

Traditionally, we have been taught to write in cursive or manuscript, using both uppercase and lowercase letters. However, when a message is to be displayed for others to see, certain approaches work best.

*Uppercase letters*, or capitals, work better for distant viewing. The letters appear clearer since they are all the same height. They are more legible. Your eye can see PEACE HOPE JOY easier from a distance than Happiness or Hooray. Uppercase letters demand at-

51

tention. They are strong and suggest that the message is important. They have a solid and demanding look.

*Lowercase letters* work better on banners viewed at close range. However, some letters are taller than others and cause your eyes to have difficulty focusing on

Illustration 21: Examples of letter types

the ups and downs of the shapes. Your mind has to work a little harder at deciphering the message. Lowercase lettering does not demand the same attention as does uppercase. It is less formal. Children's messages or greeting messages work well in lowercase as do messages that consist of one word.

*Mixed letters*, uppercase and lowercase letters used together, have their place on certain kinds of banners. Although not recommended for use on large banners, they work well for medium- to small-scale banners. Mixed lettering can appear happy and lighthearted. If the message or the occasion is celebratory, this style can project that feeling.

When you mix uppercase with lowercase lettering, your design can be abstract or puzzle-like. In this method, the written message is created by placing letters in a puzzle-like way, which will create a unique focal point for the audience to read. Since it is abstract, the viewer will have to look longer to understand the message. But in this way it entertains the viewer's attention. This placement has to be done carefully or the message will be lost. You want the viewer to be entertained, not worn out from reading it.

On smaller banners, this puzzle-like approach can solve placing the message into irregular places. When spacing is limited due to an irregular shape of the banner or an irregular space due to the shape of the symbol, the use of uppercase and lowercase lettering can double the amount of lettering possibilities. This is an abstract style.

## Positioning of Letters

In any of these lettering possibilities, the placement of your message is important. All three possibilities can be placed horizontally, vertically, diagonally, or sideways.

*Horizontal placement* reads the best and therefore is used the most. Eyes read from left to right easily since they have been trained to do so. Horizontal placement on a banner requires words that are not too long and that are the right proportionate size to prevent any run-off letters. Even on wide banners, you might have to choose a typeface that works well for length and legibility. Horizontal placement on banners can turn a simple message of farewell into a parade! (See Illustration 22.) It can be used for any message, and the layout can be designed quickly.

*Vertical placements* are harder to read since our eyes are not accustomed to reading from top to bottom. Although our eyes can shift vertically without too much confusion, it does require more reading time. If the banner is processed, have the holder walk at a slower pace so the viewer has more time to read the message. (See Illustration 23.)

Illustration 22: Horizontal placement

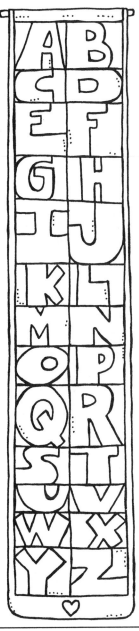

Illustration 23:
Vertical placement

Vertical placement can be used effectively with short words. You can stack the letters vertically in an entertaining pattern. In Illustration 18, the written message consists of words stacked upon one another. Imagine it being constructed in brightly colored felt so the message appears as an abstract work of art. Since the message is simple, the vertical layout creates an entertaining way of reading the message. Another example of vertical placement is a banner completely filled up with letters. No symbol is needed. This style is great for creating a sampler of the alphabet, your child's name, etc. It can be done in calicoes, felt, or even scraps of construction paper. You can construct one by yourself, or an entire class can take part in its construction. When you position vertically, make sure you place the letters closely together so they visually flow together.

*Diagonal placement* can be flattering to the total design. Beauty contests have always placed diagonal sashes around their candidates because they are flattering to their figures.

Diagonal lettering is used readily, although two challenges exist for achieving a good design.

First, should you place the diagonal message in the center of the banner? If the message reads from the upper left to the lower right, it will visually cut the banner in half. The space left in the upper right corner and lower left corner have to be filled carefully. With diagonal placement, the lettering will take up the center space where a symbol might have been placed. The leftover space is now smaller and divided. This can work well if a message can be symbolized in two parts.

Second, will viewers be able to read the diagonal message? The eye is used to reading left to right, but it must read the diagonal lettering from top to bottom, as in vertical placement. If the message is long and the lettering small, viewers might have to tilt their heads to read the message. If viewers must strain to read the banner, they might not put much effort into receiving its message. If you use this style, keep the message down to one or a few words. Also, diagonal lettering does not necessarily have to be from top left to bottom right. It can be a smaller diagonal. In Illustration 24, the diagonals are smaller and somewhat horizontal. This allows more space for words or a symbol. This is a comfortable blend of diagonal and horizontal.

*Sideways placement* of a message gives it a less dominant role in the total design. However, the impact of both the symbol and the lettering creates a strong message.

In Illustration 25, there are no symbols on the banner. The artist intended to keep the message somber;

therefore, the banner is very plain. The message is a common Bible verse; viewers' do not need to look at it intensely because with a quick scan, they will easily recognize it. The banner provides thoughts of hope and salvation. It is a support banner for those who already agree with its statement.

Your banner's size and shape are the first things you will decide on. Then you will decide upon the placement and balance of symbol and lettering. Now, let us discover how to make the letters and where to find different styles of lettering to add to our collection.

Illustration 24: Diagonal placement

Illustration 25: Sideways placement

# Typefaces

Let us consider for a moment the numerous styles of lettering and where you can find the perfect styles for your banners.

First you need to do a lot of observation. Our nation is packed with signs and billboards on our streets, in and on public transportation vehicles, as well as in our newspapers and magazines. Keep your eyes open to what style catches your attention. Create a file of clippings from magazines and newspaper ads. Although you won't have a complete alphabet for each style, you will have enough letters to create an entire alphabet. With your clippings you can create a poster displaying all the styles you find. Hang this near your work table, where you can study the shapes and keep certain styles within easy access.

Another excellent resource is a book on lettering or typefaces. Calligraphy books are readily available, and they offer an excellent variety of traditional and modern typefaces. You can purchase these books or photocopy your favorite styles from library books. Catalog books from art stores contain hundreds of typeface samples for letter transfers and rub-ons. You do not need to purchase the rub-on letters; it is the catalog that is important to you.

If your resources are limited, you can use more traditional methods of lettering. Their impact on the audience can be just as exciting as the previously mentioned ways. Stencils and patterns are the most popular method. A stencil is a tagboard sheet where the letters are cut out. (See Illustration 26.) To use the letters, you simply place the tagboard over your fabric and trace along the inner edge. I recommend that you mark your fabric on the backside, copying your letter backwards, thereby keeping the front side of the fabric clean of any markings. You can purchase these stencils at drug stores and office supply stores for a low price. They come in a variety of sizes and quality styles.

The pattern method also uses a tagboard, except instead of a cut-out opening on a sheet of paper, the stencil is the shape of the letter. These stencils are used like a pattern. They work better for me because I can lay them out on my banner background and check it for size and spacing. You can buy these, too, at office and school supply stores. Teachers use them primarily for bulletin board letters. They come in many

Illustration 26: Stencil, pattern, and freestyle lettering

sizes and shapes. The letters can be positioned onto an actual-size pattern or used directly as a pattern for cutting out your fabric. Once again, I recommend tracing on the backside of the fabric with the stencil backwards.

Another way of forming your letters is to sketch them free-hand onto your paper layout. This would be for abstract letters formed around certain designs. You can do this on graph paper, then when an actual-size pattern is made, you can cut the letters out of the layout and use them as a pattern.

Are one of those gifted people who can sit down with a pair of scissors and fabric and snip away, creating beautiful letters without any pattern or stencil at all? If you think so, experiment with newspaper to find out before attempting it with expensive fabric. If you are not satisfied with your attempt, use the other methods to achieve a professional look. It is worth your time and energy to invest in stencils and patterns for all your banners. The stencil or pattern methods are highly recommended for use with felt because it does not unravel. However, other fabrics can be used. The letters can be attached to the banner through applique, gluing, sewing, or heat bonding.

# 3.
# THE WORKING TOOLS

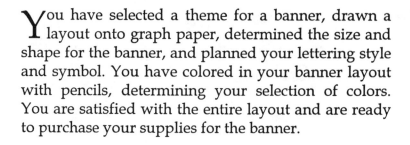

You have selected a theme for a banner, drawn a layout onto graph paper, determined the size and shape for the banner, and planned your lettering style and symbol. You have colored in your banner layout with pencils, determining your selection of colors. You are satisfied with the entire layout and are ready to purchase your supplies for the banner.

# *Fabric*

Just as it was challenging to choose your banner's shape, so will be choosing the fabric. There are so many kinds of fabric, it can be overwhelming!

When considering fabric choices, keep in mind that fabric is not just flat cloth. It has texture, which is an added element to your banner. Fabric can be slick, rough, smooth, stiff, coarse, soft, plush, lumpy, thick, thin, and transparent. Fabric can be full of designs or plain. It can stretch and pucker or can hold it shape extremely well. Fabric can be torn, cut, stuffed, overlapped, and zigzagged onto your background. In choosing your fabric, consider how different fabrics can create different feelings, even if the design is the same.

When choosing your background fabric, consider its weight. It should hold its shape and hang neatly. It should be able to hold other fabric on top of it without causing it to sag or tear. Felt and other heavyweight fabrics are ideal for backgrounds.

There are seven main categories of fabric to consider before buying.

## Felt

The most common fabric for banners is felt. Felt has the perfect weight for retaining its shape and its hanging ability. Felt is easy to cut without worrying about raw edges and raveling. You can sew or glue felt without creating a big mess. In fact, different textures can be created by sewing onto felt (by hand or machine), tearing it, gluing it, or using different stitches when you sew with it. Felt comes in a multitude of solid colors.

## Burlap

Burlap is another common background fabric. It is low priced, which helps when a large number of banners need to be made. Burlap comes in many colors. It ravels easily, which can work to your advantage if you incorporate ravels in your banner as fringes. The loosely woven strings can be pulled both vertically and horizontally to create interesting designs. Burlap is a bit more difficult to work with, as it can be scratchy and it does possess an oily smell.

## Cotton

Cotton fabric comes in many weights and textures. The Amish use this fabric and its bright colors against black backgrounds to create beautifully designed quilts. Their use of solid cotton can inspire banner makers. You can find heavy cotton canvas, ideal for background fabric. Lightweight cotton is good for applique and quilt-like banners. Batting can be added between the front and back pieces and quilted in beautiful stitching.

The colors in cotton are rich, but the dye can fade in the sunlight, so consider where the banner will hang before you purchase the material.

## Linen and Wool

Wool and linen are wonderful fabrics to work with because of their quality. These are more costly, but for close viewing your audience is sure to appreciate the quality of fabric as well as the time you put into making the banner.

Many ancient banners were made of linen, which comes in both light and heavy weights. The colors are deep and natural looking. Linen and wool create quality banners. These two fabrics are not recommended for washing, and banners made of these should be handled with care.

## Leather

Banners can be made out of leather and suede. Leather (real or fake) can create a waterproof banner ideal for rain or shine. Lightweight leather or suede can be machine sewn. Beads can be added to create a rugged or Indian appearance, which would be great for a camp, family retreat, or outdoor workshop. Dyed leather as well as assorted weights are now available. Leather can be cut, torn, and zigzagged. You may be able to find scraps sold at a low price from leather craft shops. If leather is not available for you, purchase a similar fabric like vinyl.

## Knits

Knits are used especially on 3-dimensional banners such as dolls. Knits can be used on a hanging banner when you want to stuff parts of it. You can create tassels easily by simply tearing off strips. Knits won't unravel. They come in a variety of colors, prints, and weights. Since knits stretch, cut them along the grain of the fabric.

## Silk

Silks are beautiful. Silks offer adequate stiffness while displaying shininess and glamour. The heavier silks are excellent for background fabric, while lighter weighted silk can be appliqued onto the background. Lightweight silk strips make perfect flowing touches to the sides of banners. You can paint on silk with fabric paint to create an impressive appearance. The price ranges from moderate to expensive, but the quality is unique.

There are some fabrics that do not work for background material. However, they may look and work well within the banner design. Consider lightweight transparent crepe. Overlapping the fabric can create a soft new color, great for rainbows, sunsets, and butterfly wings. More glamorous fabrics that sparkle and shine can captivate your attention as they dazzle your eyes. Sequined fabric, metallic fabric, and netting are some possibilities.

Of course, lace and trimmings can add decorations to certain areas on your banner. They can be sewn on in a straight line or in a circular fashion, or they can cover an entire area.

Search the fabric stores before deciding on your fabric. Always keep a lookout for new material. You can even find different felts in stores that carry more abundant muted colors than other stores. Know which stores carry your style of supplies. Be sure to check the scrap tables for those small but beautiful accent pieces. You can usually buy these scraps of fabric at a reduced price.

There are no rights and wrongs about fabric. If you are a beginner, I suggest working with felt. With felt you don't have to worry about grain and raveling. It cuts easily, handles well, and is easy to hand or machine sew. Once you feel confident, you can begin to experiment with different fabrics.

# Paper

Often, banners are made for a one-time affair, and these beautiful banners end up hanging in a closet, never to be seen again. With all the time and money put into the banner, it is a shame for it to become lost with the rest of the forgotten banners. In addition, many banners become out of style over the years. If your organization already has an abundance of fabric banners or the occasion for your banner is a one-time affair, you might want to make your banner out of paper.

Why spend a lot of money and time when a banner can be made with paper and paint? From a distance, no one can tell the difference. Large banners in a convention hall or banners that hang in front of the church are ideal candidates for paper.

Some of you readers may think paper banners will be too plain or cheap. However, with the paper products available to us today, paper banners can be quite ornate. The possibilities include butcher paper, colored paper rolls that are used for bulletin boards, rolls of fadeless paper, foil, wrapping paper, posterboard, paper streamers, construction paper, and more.

The interior part of a paper banner can also be made out of paper. The lettering is easier to cut because there is no grain to consider. Paper letters and symbols handle easier and can be glued down instead of sewn on, or you can give the paper banner some depth by raising the lettering and symbol with foamboard or cardboard beneath the raised areas. This works well and looks great on a heavier background board such as posterboard of heavier weight.

Besides cutting out the lettering and symbols, you can also paint them directly on to the posterboard. It might seem as though you are simply making a poster, and in a way you are. However, when you hang it or process it, it becomes a glorious banner, crisp and strong. Tempera paint works best and is least expensive. Most schools have an assortment of colors, or you can purchase your own paint from local school supply stores. Your choice of colors ranges from the primary colors to a complete rainbow of colors, including fluorescent colors.

In the past, I taught art at a school where I was responsible for creating a hallway banner each month. I always used a roll of colored bulletin board paper and tempera paint. It hung well, and the colors remained bright and clear. Sometimes I combined glitter and other materials to draw attention. Paper banners work well because of the time and cost element. If you have an area where you want to have changing banners, I suggest this method. It works well for the narthex of a church, entrance to a preschool, or outside your classroom door for announcing the theme of the week. Streamers can be attached in the same way as on cloth banners, and the movement will catch attention. These posterboard banners are easily stored and can be used year after year. You can change streamers to feathers and bells the year after to create an all-new look.

In planning your paper banner, you can draw your layout directly on your paper. There is no need for pattern-making. Simply erase the pencil marking when you are finished, and you are ready to hang your banner.

Before hanging your banner, you need to create an opening to slip a rod through. You can do this in two ways. If your banner is made out of lightweight paper, simply turn back three inches along the top of the banner. Glue or staple the paper down. If your banner is out of posterboard, take six inches of lightweight paper that is the same width of your banner, fold it in half lengthwise, and attach it to the top of the banner with glue or staples. You can also use transparent fishing line. Make a small hole on the top corners of the board and tie the banner into place on the pole. (See Illustration 27.)

I've also seen banners made out of paper interfacing, which you can purchase at fabric stores. It is a paper-fabric blend that comes on a bolt with a good width for a banner. The interfacing material is great for painting on your lettering and symbols, yet it appears to have the softness of fabric.

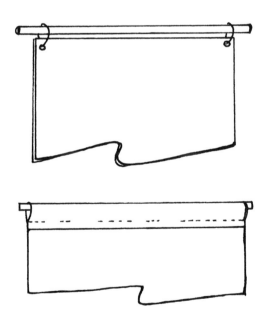

Illustration 27: Posterboard banners

4.

PUTTING
IT
TOGETHER

Before you begin to plan and construct a banner, you need to gather all the important information so the banner's purpose is clear to you. More than likely someone has approached you with that information. Perhaps they have provided the message that is to appear on a banner, and maybe the date when they would like it to be completed. However, there is much more information that the artist needs before she can begin. The questionnaire on the opposite page serves as a checklist whenever I am approached to make a banner. In fact, I have copies of this checklist and use it much as a notepad. The minute I am asked to make a banner, I begin to fill out the information. Sometimes the person requesting the banner does not know some of the answers and needs to ask another for the facts. In the end, when your checklist is completed, you can refer to it and know you are headed in the right direction.

The final step is the most exciting part of the entire process. Your mind has sorted through many ideas, and you have created your own design to fit your needs. Your sketch is complete, and you have made all the decisions concerning size, shapes, colors, fabric, and so on. At this point you can picture the completed banner in your mind. Now you need to gather all your materials and supplies. You will need butcher paper (or any long roll of paper) for drawing out your actual-size pattern, dark marker, scissors, pins, fabric, and threads. Find a place where you can spread everything out, such as the dining room table, a classroom work table, or even a wooden floor. For the beginning hours, you will want a place where your work can remain undisturbed because this is a long process.

1. What is the goal of the banner?

- ☐ support
- ☐ identify
- ☐ celebrate
- ☐ stir emotion
- ☐ inform

2. List any known information.

a. Required or suggested words

b. Required or suggested symbol(s)

c. Required or suggested color(s)

d. Required or suggested size

3. What is the theme of the occasion?

4. Where will the banner be displayed?

5. Is it to be processed or permanent?

6. What fabric will best support the message?

- ☐ Felt
- ☐ Canvas
- ☐ Silk
- ☐ Linen
- ☐ Burlap
- ☐ Paper

7. Date for sketch to be turned in for approval _____

8. Date for banner to be completed _____

Once you have organized your fabric and working tools, you will work out the construction. (See Illustration 28). You can work directly from an actual-size pattern or work from your original sketch. The latter-mentioned is for the more advanced person. The first process is the more practical and easier process to work through.

Illustration 28: Work area for banner making

# Enlarging Your Sketch

Your sketch is finalized and you are happy with its shape and design. Therefore, you are ready to enlarge your design to create an actual-size pattern from which you can cut and place your fabric.

There are two ways of enlarging your banner design. The first way involves access to an overhead projector and a sheet of acetate paper. If you have access to a school, you should be able to find these supplies in the office. You can simply take the sheet of acetate and trace over your design with overhead markers or a small permanent marker. Lay your traced acetate sheet on the projector and hang a large strip of paper on a wall or bulletin board. With your design projected onto the paper, simply trace over it. You may have to move the projector around or adjust the focus to create the correct size you planned for your banner.

There is a quicker and more precise method for duplicating your design onto an acetate sheet. Draw your design on regular paper with a dark marker. Put it in a copy machine, but instead of copying it onto regular paper, copy it onto the sheet of acetate. You will receive a perfect copy of your design, which will project clearly on the wall. You can also enlarge or reduce your design if the copier has this function.

If you do not have access to these machines, you can use another method. It requires more time but works just as well. To begin, take your sketch and clearly distinguish your banner size. If you have drawn out your design onto graph paper, this step will have already been done. In this case, you will decide on a proper proportion and increase the dimensions. For example, if your sketch is 3" x 5", you can determine your actual-size banner to be 3' x 5', using a ratio of one inch to one foot (1" = 1'). On your large paper, you would draw the outside dimensions (3' x 5'), then mark off the fifteen square feet within.

Here is a quicker method that accomplishes the same thing and can be used if you did not draw your design out on graph paper. Lightly divide your design in half, both vertically and horizontally, by drawing over your design with a pencil. This divides the sketch into fourths. If your design is big, you may wish to divide in into eighths. Now draw your actual banner size onto your large paper. The banner size must be proportionate to your original sketch. You can multiply the sketch size by any number, as long as you are consistent with all sides. Finally, using light pencil, divide your drawn banner into halves and then fourths, in the same places as on your sketch. These guidelines must be proportionate to the sketch's marks. (The lines on your paper will not be permanent; they are just to guide your enlarging process. When the process is complete, erase them.)

Now you are ready to begin to copy from your sketch onto your paper. If you wish, you can lightly number your boxes to prevent getting mixed up when copying. Do this on both your sketch and on your enlarged banner. Begin at the top left-hand corner. Draw any lines that appear in that box into the enlarged box. Look carefully and continue throughout all your boxes, making sure that the proper lines meet at the correct places from one box to another. Make adjustments when the lines are not meeting. This process may take a few minutes or an hour, depending on how simple or complicated your design is. When completed, go over your new banner enlargement

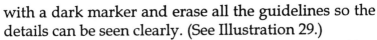

with a dark marker and erase all the guidelines so the details can be seen clearly. (See Illustration 29.)

Now you have an enlarged actual-size pattern. You can either copy and cut from it as a pattern, or you can use it merely as a guide for your placement of details. I call these two options direct pattern transfer and indirect pattern transfer.

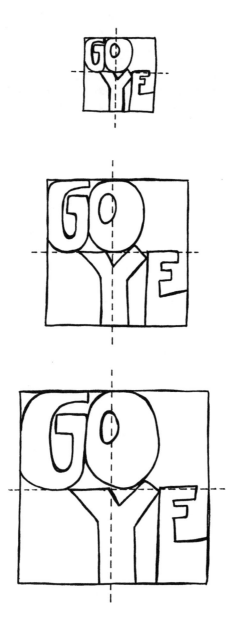

Illustration 29: Enlarging your banner

# Direct Pattern Transfer

Some disciplined artists plan out every detail of their banner and expect it to look just like their planned sketch. They do not allow anything on their banner to differ from the original sketch. Direct pattern transfer is the method of using the enlarged banner design pattern directly on your fabric.

Begin your banner by cutting out the background piece first, using the enlarged pattern as a guide. Then cut out the lettering and symbol from the enlarged pattern and lay these on top of the fabric you're using for designs. As mentioned in an earlier chapter, it is advisable to place your pattern backward on the backside of the fabric, so if you draw around your pattern the marks will not show. Turn over the cutout pieces and place them directly onto your background fabric. Pin into place. Continue this process until all the details have been cut out and positioned on the banner. When everything is in the correct position, you can begin to sew or glue each piece down permanently. (See Illustration 30.)

This process works quickly because you have made all your decisions beforehand, and now all you have to do is to cut out the pieces and place them in position.

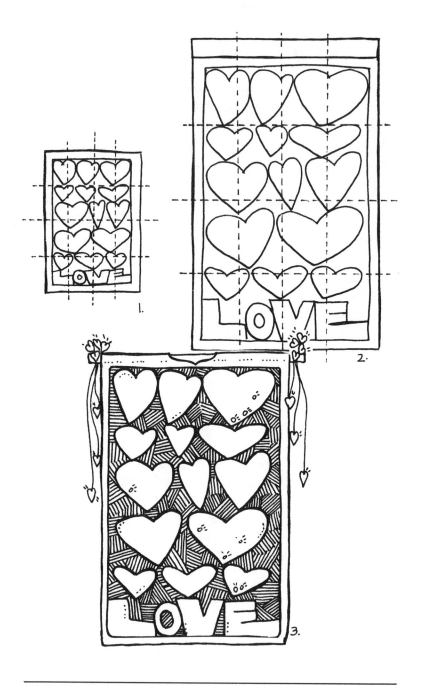

Illustration 30: Direct pattern transfer

# Indirect Pattern Transfer

Some artists get anxious to start on the construction of their banner and trust their instincts enough to leave the creating part to the snipping and arranging of the fabric. Indirect pattern transfer offers the artist that freedom by using the sketch as an idea starter and leaving the arranging to inspiration.

In this process the artists does not necessarily draw out an enlarged sketch. Looking at the sketch, the artist uses that as a guide, allowing for some creative changes along the way. The original sketch may not look exactly like the finished banner. It might be more creative and exciting than previously planned! (See Illustration 31.)

In this process you might take more time playing around with different possibilities. This method is not as rigid as the direct pattern transfer. In fact, you might take a couple of days to work out the positioning of the lettering and symbols, or you might come up with a completely new look.

Each artist must decide which method works well for herself. I have used both methods. When I'm making a banner with precise orders from the organization, I work with the direct pattern transfer. In this situation, making the banner is more of a business order and therefore a business-like relationship must be maintained. However, when I'm the designer of the banner, I create along the way, even up to the last step. I use my sketch carefully, but I don't let it keep me from any last-moment inspiration. This allows for more fun.

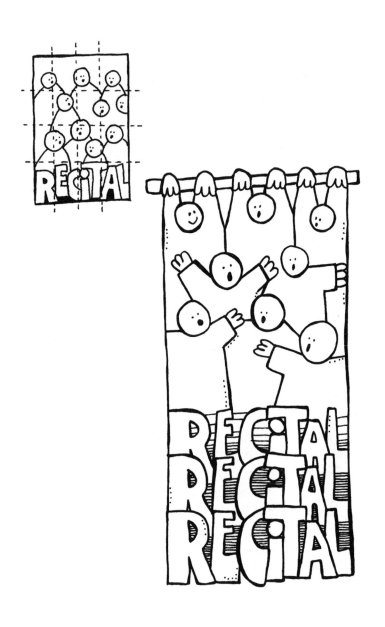

Illustration 31: Indirect pattern transfer

# Adhering

There are many ways of adhering your designs to a background for permanent bonding. Certain techniques involve time and extra supplies. Some artists use a combination of adhering methods on one banner, depending on the materials used.

## Glue

The most common method used throughout the years is using white glue. White glue bonds heavier fabrics as well as paper objects. It is usually an inexpensive supply that most households have readily available. However, it does have some disadvantages. First, if the glue is not put on heavily enough and close enough to the edge, the fabric can fall off with the slightest movement. If the glue is applied too heavily, the glue may leak through the fabric, causing a crusty clear surface on the front of the banner. If the glue is too close to the edge of the fabric and you want to sew around the edges, you will have difficulty pushing the needle through. My solution is to purchase a white glue designed for use on fabric. It is thick but dries into a soft bonding material. It dries clear and works great with felt.

Hot glue is becoming more popular. It is a hard glue inserted in a gun-like tool that heats the glue to a thick tacky substance. It glues thick fabric, such as felt, securely and quickly. It works great for surface decorations as well. You can purchase glue and hot-glue guns in craft, fabric, and hardware stores.

## Heat Bonding

Another process for adhering fabric is the use of a heat-bonding fabric. This is a lightweight, paper-like material that can be cut to the exact size and shape of your letters and designs. Place it between your letters and backing, use an iron to press the heat through the layers, and the heat-bonding material will fuse the fabrics together. The process works quickly and adheres well. Once the design is in place, you can sew through it easily, if desired. This process requires accurate placement because letters cannot be repositioned once they are fused. You can purchase this material at fabric stores. The most common brand is called Stitch Witchery.

## Hand or Machine Sewing

I enjoy hand or machine sewing the lettering and design in place. This method creates a thicker appearance of the fabric (especially felt). Hand sewing gives a soft, plump look to the designs and rounds off the edge of the thickness of the fabric. Machine sewing works well, especially on small banners. It's the maneuvering of the fabric under the machine that requires talent. But the effect on the textures is worth the struggle. Machine stitching gives the banner a thick texture with sharp blunt edges. If you sew over every detail without lifting and repositioning the needle, it creates a child-like look appropriate for banners for children or with a simple message. I usually heat bond my letters and designs on first, then go back over the letters and designs by either hand or machine stitching.

# 5.
# BANNER
# FINISHES
## TOP
## BOTTOM
## PROCESSIONAL
## SIGNATURES

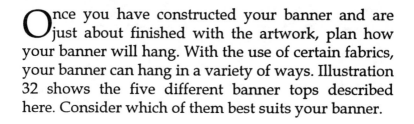

Once you have constructed your banner and are just about finished with the artwork, plan how your banner will hang. With the use of certain fabrics, your banner can hang in a variety of ways. Illustration 32 shows the five different banner tops described here. Consider which of them best suits your banner.

# Banner Tops

If your banner is made out of burlap or any loosely woven fabric, you may finish the top of the banner by slipping a rod through the strings of burlap a few inches from the top. Some threads will have to be cut to allow the rod to slip through.

Another finishing method for the top of a banner is to simply turn back the top edge far enough over so a rod can slip through the allowance. You can hot glue the fabric together or machine stitch it. Be sure that the closure is strong enough to hold the weight of the banner.

A third way is to turn the top fabric over toward the front of the banner. This creates a scroll effect, great for a paper banner. Once again, make sure the top is secure so it will not tear or become unattached.

To make a banner of good weight hang nicely, you can use two thicknesses of fabric. I often use this method when I work with felt. It adds the right amount of weight and looks good. After making your banner, cut out a piece of fabric from the same fabric you used for the background. (You can use a different color fabric if your banner has some cutout windows and you want another color to show through behind the cutouts.) This piece should be the same width as your banner but long enough to double over the top of it. Lay this piece behind the banner and machine or hand sew it, sewing a side first, then the bottom, then the other side. Sew no farther than one-quarter inch away from the edge. Turn the top edge over toward the front or back and stitch down, allowing enough room for a rod.

Another method is the pocket method. This is great for lightweight fabric because it will finish off the edges nicely and it will add weight to the banner. In this method you cut out an identical backing shape to your banner. Lay the finished banner and the backing right sides together. Sew around the sides and bottom. Turn right sides out and press. Turn the top edge seam allowance under and sew shut. Turn the top either to the front or the back and stitch down, leaving enough space to slip a rod through.

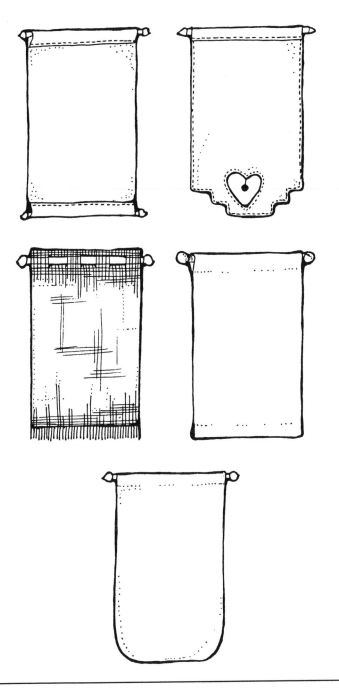

Illustration 32: Banner tops

# Banner Rods

There are many exciting possibilities for rods, some as near as your backyard and some as far as your local hardware store. You need not go to great expense for your rod, but you should have an appropriate rod for displaying your banner. Illustration 33 shows the different kinds of rods described here.

Remember, the purpose of a rod is to hold your banner out straight. There are many materials for that. One could be a small branch. The branch needs to be straight and strong enough to hold the weight of the banner. This works great if your banner has a rugged appearance or is made with rugged materials like burlap.

Another rod, and the most common, is a dowel. You can purchase dowels at craft and hardware stores. Dowels come in a variety of thicknesses. Be sure to purchase a dowel that is strong enough to hold your banner's weight.

If you have scraps of piping or tubing, you can use them as rods. You can buy plastic piping called PVC at hardware stores.

You can also use wood strips. Cut them the width of the banner and attach them to the top front and top back of the banner.

A rod should be the same width as the banner. In some cases you may wish to extend the rods an inch on both sides of the banner. Take a look at Illustration 40 and determine which will work best for you.

If your banner is to hang from a banner stand or even on the wall, you will need to attach a string from each side of the rod. The string can be made of twine, ribbon, cording, braided yarn, or leather. The length of the string should allow for tying on each end of the rod. Some banners can hang with the rod attached to the banner stand. In this case, there is no need for string.

Depending on the rod you choose, you can attach the string to the rods in a variety of ways. (See Illustration 34.) A simple metal hook or loop can be screwed into a dowel, allowing the string to be attached to the hooks.

With wooden rods, you can carve out depressions to tie your string around. This will allow the string to stay in place and not slip off the ends.

If a saw is available, you can cut an inch or two into each edge of a wooden dowel. Tie fancy knots at the

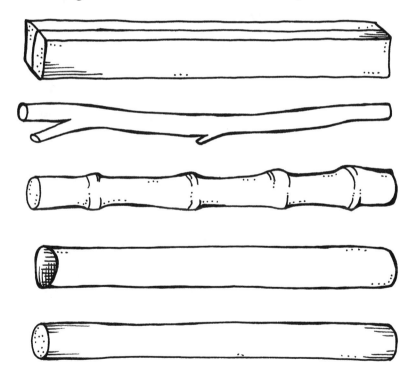

Illustration 33: Banner rods

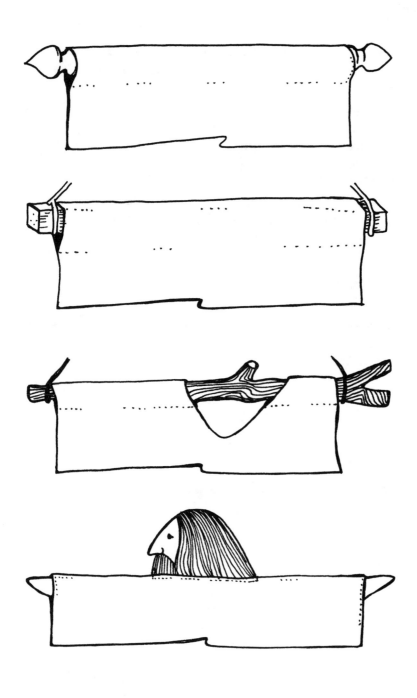

Illustration 34: Attachments

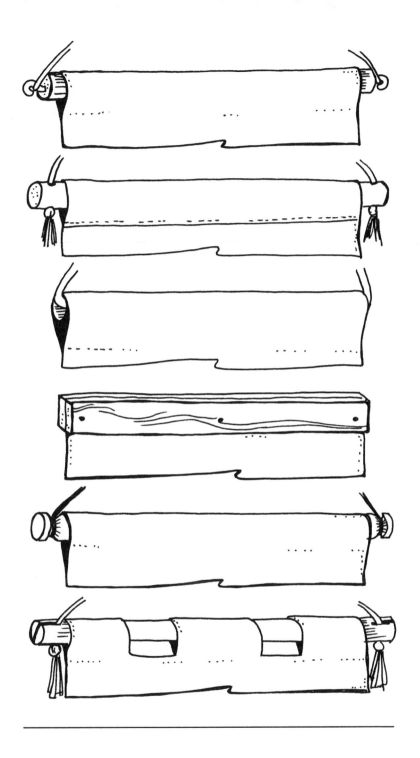

ends of the string and slip into the cuts with the knots below the rod. The knots will hold the string in place.

If you have chosen piping, allow enough string to run through it and tie together.

Plain or fancy curtain rods can be used. Smaller and thinner curtain rods have holes at the end where you can slip in your string. The larger, more decorative rods require the string to be tied onto the rod.

If you use the branch method, choose one to fit your banner's style. For example, if your banner has cuts in the top edge, try to find a branch with small twigs growing out of it. Slip the banner over the branch so the twigs poke out of the openings in your banner's top edge.

Your rod can be as decorative as the banner itself and work together as one unit. Your rod can be carved or cut with a saw, perhaps in the shape of a tree or a person's head with outstretched arms. The banner would then be placed over the shoulders, creating a piece of clothing effect. This is an interesting way to display permanently hanging banners along a wall.

# Banner Bottoms

Most banners hang best when the bottom of the banner is weighted slightly or finished off with some heavy details. This not only helps the banner hang nicely but allows a more finished appearance.

If you have used burlap for the banner background, you may simply unravel several inches of the bottom rows to create a nice fringe. This can be done with other loosely woven fabrics as well. It is a quick but interesting finish for your banner.

If your fabric does not unravel easily, you can purchase many kinds of trim for the lower edge. From fringes to pom pons, you will find an assortment of colors and styles.

Many banners are simply finished with a fancy cut at the bottom. Or the banner has been sewn in a pocket fashion. If you intend your banner to remain simple, no further decoration or weight is needed.

Some banners that have a straight bottom edge may not hang evenly and blow over when it is processed. You may wish to turn over the bottom edge and slip a dowel through in the same way as you would the top edge. This will allow the banner to hang flat. (See Illustration 32.)

# Finishing Touches

Your banner is finished. You have carefully pressed it, and it is hanging nicely on its rod. You have worked hard on the design, and your craftsmanship is of the best quality. Before turning it over to the organization you made it for, live with the banner for a while. Look at it often. If every time you look at it, it still gives you a satisfied feeling, then it is ready to send it on its way. If, however, you begin to loose that satisfied feeling, there are some last-minute touches you can put on your banner.

Many times even the most beautiful banner remains a bit dull. Here the artist needs to take a careful look and add some touches to make it stimulating to its audience. One method is to add some surface decorations. (See Illustration 35.)

Beads are one kind of surface decoration that works effectively on a banner. If your banner is to be seen at a close range, it truly calls for some attention! There are the traditional Indian beads that measure ⅛". Larger beads come in all sorts of colors, even metallic. You can also buy wooden, clay, and plastic beads, usually used for macrame. If you know how, you can make your own beads out of clay. These beads can be sewn on or applied with a hot-glue gun.

Sequins work well, especially if your message has a sparkling and joyous message. I have used sequins on tiny banners using ¼" sequins as well as one-inch sequins on large, convention hall banners. Here the light, whether the banner is permanently mounted on a wall or processed, will dazzle and dance.

Different ideas include buttons, seeds, and bells. When used on the right kind of banner and with the appropriate message, they are quite effective.

Illustration 35:
Decorations

Sometimes adding a small amount of a different fabric to your banner can finish off the appearance. Leather, felt, satin, muslin, lace, netting, and trims are just a few. If you fold or twist these fabrics in an interesting way, you can create an interesting three-dimensional look. Instead of cutting your felt, try tearing it or using a pair of zigzag scissors. You may want to open a seam on your appliqued piece and slip in a little bit of stuffing to add different layers to your banner. When the lights shine on the banner, it will create shadows on the surface.

Sometimes your banner just needs a few added stitches to enhance its details. French knots are a popular decoration for any banner. Consult embroidery books for more fancy stitches.

Glitter also calls attention to your banner. You can buy glitter in different sizes and in different mediums. Nowadays, glitter, called angel dust, can be found in a liquid. It is brushed on, dries clear, but allows tiny glitter

99

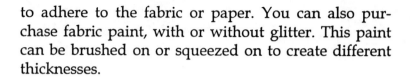

to adhere to the fabric or paper. You can also purchase fabric paint, with or without glitter. This paint
can be brushed on or squeezed on to create different
thicknesses.

# Processional Banners

When your banner is complete, slip it onto the rod and take a good look at it.

If the banner is to be a processional banner, movement will be important to its message. Since the banner will be processed, you may wish to add some exciting elements to intensify the movement. Decorations for movement can be added to the surface of the banner, the rods of the banner, and the lower edge of the banner. (See Illustration 36.)

Ribbons are an excellent material to embellish the rods of a banner. You can attach the ribbons by tying tiny bows at the top of each rod's end or by simply wrapping them around the rods a bit before letting them dangle. (If you intend to use ribbons at the end of the rods, cut the rods several inches longer than the width of the banner.) Different widths and lengths will create assorted movements in the air. Thinner ribbon flutters easier, while wider ribbon floats through the air. Ribbons can be one color or a rainbow of colors. If your banner is made out of paper, you can use curling ribbon or paper ribbons.

Other items that can be attached to rods are feathers, pom pons, colorful yarns, or a combination of the above. They can be tightly attached at the ends of the rods or dangle loosely down in several layers.

You may want to not only stir excitement through movement from the banner but also through sound. Small bells and clangers can be attached to ribbons and along the lower edge of a banner. Larger bells make an impressive ring, while smaller bells sing a sweet song.

Clangers can be made out of small tin can lids. Save the tin lids that have been cut off with a can opener.

Illustration 36: Decorations for processional banners

Very carefully, use pliers to twist the lid to form a cone. Tie a hardware nut to a string for a dangler, then tie another knot an inch or so above the nut. Slip the string through the cone lid until the first knot hits the top. Tie another knot on the outside so the string cannot be pulled either way. The clangers can be hung one by one or in a cluster.

Clangers can also be made from frozen juice container lids, which have safe thick edges. When several lids are hung close together so that they hit each other, they make a delightful sound. The flat, circular, inner surface can be painted or lined with fabric. Just keep the edges clear of fabric. Punch a hole in the inner rim and tie with string or ribbon.

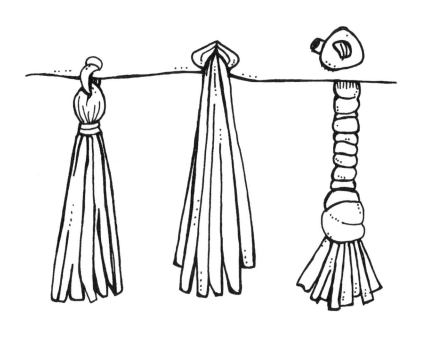

Small metal or plastic containers, such as spice containers or prescription medicine containers, make great noise makers. Simply fill the containers with a few pebbles and seal shut. Hot glue or wrap the containers in yarn and attach to the banner's edge. (See Illustration 37.)

One other idea is to use a bit of potpourri in your banner. As it is processed, the message is brought to your audience's attention not only through sight and sound but also through smell. This does not mean spray your banner with a heavily scented perfume. It does mean that a gentle scent can leave a lingering impression on your audience. One way is to dot on a few drips of essence oil before your banner is processed. You can also prepare your own potpourri recipe and

make a small pouch for it. Sew the pouch on the back
corner or perhaps you can use it on the front message
of your banner.

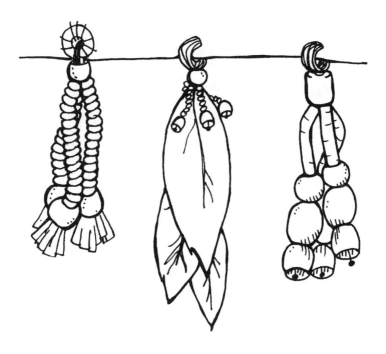

Illustration 37: Clangers

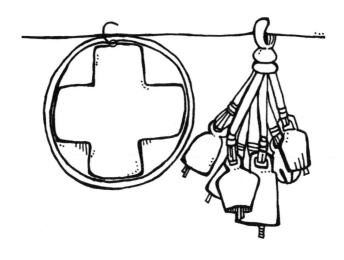

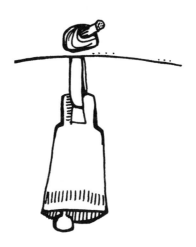

# Your Signature

Now that your banner is completely finished, your final seal of approval is to put your signature on the banner. Too often, beautiful banners are created and the artist stays anonymous. All works of art should be claimed by the artist, though in no way does it mean that your name needs to be plastered all over the backside of your banner.

When I started making banners, I never attached my name to the banner. The people who see them now do not know who made the banner and what part I played in the church at that time. Sure, the glory of a church banner should go to God, but signing it tells people that you have used your God-given talents. For other organizations, I feel putting my name on the banner is my calling card for future references.

Let's take a look at the many ways you can sign your name on your banner. Illustration 38 shows some of the signatures described here.

The most common way is to simply write your name on the back edge of the banner with a pen. A laundry or Sharpie pen works the best. If you use a textured fabric or felt, you will find that the pen does not print clearly. An option to that is to write your name on a piece of smooth fabric and then attach that fabric to the lower edge of the back side.

Historically, many quilters embroidered their name onto their quilt with colorful thread. This can also be done to your signature. Rainbow embroidery thread or a color that has some meaning to you should be used. You can embroider your whole name or just your initials. Some quilts have been found with the name embroidered from the quilter's hair.

Illustration 38:
Signatures

Some artists really think about their style of signature and want to express something about themselves in that signature. Some Christian artists attach a seed that has their initials marked on it. The seed has a hole drilled through and is attached with thread. Other artists use a small pearl or a small cross.

Some artists make their own clay beads and stamp their symbol or signature into it. Purchased beads can also be used. I have seen small bells with initials on it.

My signature consists of a tiny shell. I lived in Florida for ten years and enjoyed collecting seashells. Some of my collection were simple white scallops with natural small holes in them. Most people would not want these, but I thought they were perfect. Inside the shell I wrote my name, the date, and a PX symbol. I then attached the shell to the banner with gold thread. I have continued this method throughout the years.

Whatever way you sign your banner, you should feel

it fully expresses your style. Use it confidently and thankfully. It says that you care about the message the banner expresses and that you have used your talents well to help others understand it. Use your signature as an approval of the message and of your work. For if you succeed in being proud of your work, you are truly an artist.

DIANE

diane guelzow

TAKE MY HANDS
AND LET THEM DO
WORKS THAT SHOW
MY LOVE FOR YOU

## EXTRAORDINARY BANNERS FOR ORDINARY TIMES
*George Collopy*
Paperbound, $11.95
144 pages, 6" x 9"
ISBN: 0-89390-225-X

Here are more than 100 exciting patterns from award-winning graphic artist George Collopy. This companion volume to *It's a Banner Year!* focuses on religious and secular themes for ordinary times. These classic patterns derive from Renaissance art and early American quilts. Use them as is, or adapt them for banners, embroidery, or graphics. Available March 1992.

## IT'S A BANNER YEAR!
*George Collopy*
Paperbound, $11.95
211 pages, 6" x 9"
ISBN: 0-89390-176-8

Looking for fresh banner ideas? Then you'll love these banner and temporary art designs for liturgical seasons, sacraments, and secular holidays. Designs have grid overlays for easy reproduction.

## BANNERS WITHOUT WORDS
*Jill Knuth*
Paperbound, $10.95
198 pages, 6" x 9"
ISBN 0-89390-075-3

This collection of design ideas, illustrations, instructions, and handy tips will help you make your own beautiful, wordless banners. More than 50 reproducible designs!

*"An interesting sense of symbolism...fresh images...Incorporates many innovative techniques."*
— Provident Book Finder

## BANNERS AND SUCH
*Adelaide Ortegel, S.P.*
Paperbound, $10.95
127 pages, 7" x 10"
ISBN 0-89390-092-3

A basic source of design principles for any visual construction—banners, altar cloths, vestments, antependiums, and other creative visual articles. Revised edition includes new section on environments and updated resource guide.

## USING ART IN SUNDAY WORSHIP
*Eileen Gurak*
Paperbound, $7.95, 80 pages, 5½" x 8½"
ISBN: 0-89390-186-5

This book takes the principles found in *Environment and Art in Catholic Worship* and *The General Instruction of the Roman Missal* and applies them to Sunday worship. The author distinguishes between religious and liturgical art—and shows how to decorate and organize your worship space for maximum participation. Helpful illustrations.

## LIGHT: Multimedia Techniques for Celebration
*Adelaide Ortegal, S.P., and Kent E. Schneider*
Paperbound, $10.95, 144 pages, 7" x 10"
ISBN: 0-89390-094-X

Designed to help you use combinations of photographic and creative light images to communicate your ideas, these techniques will open doors to unlimited possibilities of expression. Can be used in countless ways for school, church, and business organizations.

Order these resources through your bookseller, or use the order form on the last page.

# Put Pizazz in Your Bulletins, Stationery, and Programs, Too!

## CLIP ART for Bulletins and Beyond
*George Collopy*
Paperbound, $14.95
125 perforated pages, 8½" x 11"
ISBN 0-89390-124-5

Produce easy-to-do, eye-pleasing bulletins, banners, and programs with art appropriate for any Sunday of the liturgical year and in various sizes for your convenience. Learn how to use clip art to your best advantage, how to make different bulletins using different folds, and how to enlarge art spots to your specifications. Themes includes the Church, the resurrection, Hebrew Scripture, Jesus Christ, the Trinity, the Cross, and the Virgin Mary.

## CLIP ART for Communicating the Good News
*Jean Morningstar*
Paperbound, $14.95
128 pages perforated, 8½" x 11"
ISBN 0-89390-160-1

These drawings, a remarkable blend of simplicity and inspiration, illustrate passages from throughout the Bible, and cover the seasons of Advent, Christmas, Lent, Easter, Pentecost and many other feasts. The unique format allows you to use them "as is" or in your own designs. Great for stationery, newsletters, student handouts, Sunday bulletins, and flyers.

---